The Psalm Book of Charles Knowles

the psalm book

of charles knowles

The Pinnacle Press   New York   The Viking Press

First published in 1962 by The Viking Press, Inc. and The Pinnacle Press, Inc.
625 Madison Avenue, New York 22, N.Y.

Published simultaneously in Canada by
The Macmillan Company of Canada Ltd.

Library of Congress catalog card number: 62-17941
Text printed in U.S.A. by Hallmark Litho
Illustrations printed in Belgium by P.A.G., Ets Bindels and Weyenberg S.A.

A portion of this book appeared in McCall's magazine

Foreword

There are many reasons why the *Psalm Book* by Charles Knowles moves me. The snuffing out of any promising young life is always poignant, but it is not because of this boy's tragically premature death that I write these few words about his work; it is because he possessed the seeds of an authentic artist. I never knew Charles Knowles and I have seen no other work by him, but the *Psalm Book* alone is enough to convince me of his stature. The fact that at seventeen he was able with extraordinary perseverance to carry through each step of a complicated production is impressive, for, as Philip Hofer points out, Charles was at once the artist, designer, and printer of this publication. The fact that at seventeen he had already acquired enviable, if limited, skills in three exacting fields is also impressive, but far more impressive was his ability to project powerful emotions with the utmost simplicity.

His long illness perhaps explains a maturity and freedom of expression little known to the average teen-ager; it also may explain

5

the searching faith that characterizes every inch of this book. These eight large woodcuts illustrating Charles' favorite psalms are an object lesson in their total regard for meaning. To be sure, they do more than merely illustrate the text; they interpret it with touching fervor. The very technical limitations that restrict the prints become their advantage, for here strong, sometimes awkward draftsmanship has a primitive authority totally in harmony with the psalms themselves. Like all legitimate primitive artists, Charles Knowles was more interested in what he had to say than in how he said it. Throughout his book, emotional content forces technique to become the tool of expression, a fact that explains the stringent economy of these stark woodcuts where not an extra line or decorative frill obtrudes. Nor was this young artist trying to be original; he was, instead, set on communicating certain ideas with methods adapted to the needs of his theme.

The book's bold weighted type relates to the heavy illustrations with the same sympathy with which they in turn relate to the apocalyptic words. The entire portfolio has a unity resulting, in part, from careful planning; in part, from an intuitive sense of design; but, above all, from a devotion to the full meaning of the text. Possibly the most sensitive single element in the volume is its deliberately reserved use of color. Once again decoration is denied in favor of emotional content. Surprisingly restrained and often muted color areas become foils for occasional pure bursts of bright yellow or red. It is this over-all interrelated control of design, medium, color, and meaning that is astonishing from so young and inexperienced an artist.

We are accustomed to prodigies in music. In the visual arts early proficiency is not always a reliable omen. Obviously Charles Knowles was less a prodigy than a dedicated craftsman, but it is never his technical facility that moves us; it is his unerring ability to transform collective beliefs into concrete symbols. His drawing is faulty, in-

6

deed sometimes naive, but, as Paul Klee once sagely observed, "Much can be learned from the beginnings of art," from ethnographic collections and from the work of children. This is true of the *Psalm Book*. Though it is in no sense childish, it has the concentrated conviction of the "beginnings of art," of an art where sophisticated methods have not yet intervened to obscure or subvert the artist's intention. Clearly, Charles Knowles' intention was focused on honoring certain of man's wisest words and bravest credos. The symbols he used are often familiar, but this young artist made them very much his own. The *Psalm Book* is a testament to the power of a sensitive eye, a controlled hand, and an absorbing faith.

KATHARINE KUH
Art Editor, *Saturday Review*

charles knowles

(1939-1958)

The artist-printer of this *Psalm Book,* which is here reproduced for the first time, was born in Denver, Colorado, on August 4, 1939, the son of well-educated though not wealthy parents. Between the ages of three and six, Charles Knowles was in the Children's Hospital for a good deal of time in an unsuccessful attempt to cure the chronic nephritis with which he came into the world. The doctors finally agreed that there was nothing more that medical science could offer, and he was discharged from the hospital as a hopeless case. "According to all the books, this boy should be dead," a physician said privately. Yet he had twelve more years to live.

"I was an only child who played with grownups more than I played with children," Charles wrote in 1956. "When I did play with children, it was with a single friend. I couldn't get along in a group. I was left out of things when there were other children around. It wasn't my fault that I was left on the fringes; few of my troubles were my fault. It wasn't my fault that I had to go to the hospital. But how could I explain to other children, whose gauge of social prestige was proficiency in games, that the reason I couldn't play well was that I had been sick? I couldn't chin myself on the 'jungle gym' at the school. When a ball came to me, I seldom caught it."

Naturally such a child, at only eight years of age, became unpopular, because he was *different*—sometimes shy and sometimes garrulous. His contemporaries teased him unmercifully "with that awful instinctive psychology that children understand" (Charles Knowles' own words). In self-defense, this boy, who understood so clearly why he was plagued, soon learned to tease back, and finally how to become truly loved by his intimates. But it took years of soul-searching, patient effort. Nor does one become wholly well-adjusted after such a difficult start.

Ill health and unpopularity were not the boy's only handicaps. At the age of ten, his hearing started to fail. But by this time he had begun to fight back strongly; he studied lip-reading and rapidly became so proficient that even his new-found friends were hardly conscious that he was partly deaf. He had already learned to appreciate good music, and fortunately he kept enough hearing to enjoy all the forms of it that he loved dearly, so long as he had a chance to sit in close.

Meanwhile, the children's Saturday morning classes at the Denver Art Museum served to initiate his even stronger passion for art. A great-grandfather and a great-uncle of his had been artists. The talent must have been born in him. During the summer of 1954, when Charles Knowles was still fourteen, one of his paintings and one of his sculptures were exhibited. They were his first serious efforts in these directions.

In the autumn, when Charles was just fifteen, he set off resolutely from Denver for the East. He had been accepted in Putney School, Vermont, one of the most progressive private institutions

10

in the country. A paper that he wrote during his first few weeks, titled "The Type of Person That I Want to Be," proves how inspiringly the timid, ill-adjusted boy had developed in a few years of disciplined concentration on his personal problems. The notes of hope, determination, and enthusiasm are contagious:

The ability to live with oneself and with others is the most important thing a person can ever learn. Putney's curriculum does not include only English and Geometry, it has another lesson that a public school can never teach—how to live with others, and consequently yourself. . . . I want to be able to appreciate the other cultures, the other peoples of this world, and their contribution to [its] betterment. . . . [for] here you find people and things that come from—or have been to—nearly every place on the globe, except perhaps Antarctica and Thule. . . . I've always loved art, music. . . . I love the Friday night singing, and the Sunday night meetings for that wonderful tingling feeling in my spine that I always get when good music is played. I want to be religious, not in the usual sense, but in the sense of living a life that is good, one to be proud of—a beautiful life full of happiness for myself and others. . . . I want to be a *real* person. . . . I want friends. There is no one here that I really dislike. I only hope that people here like *me*. . . . Every life is a huge mosaic. It can be beautiful or it can be hideous. Each event in your life is a stone in the mosaic. If a person has absorbed the real and good things in life, the mosaic will be beautiful beyond imagination. . . .

Clearly Charles Knowles had come a long way, from unpopularity to acceptance, from insecurity to confidence. His mother, who wrote most of the facts hereafter recorded, perceived every step in advance; doubtless she also helped to lead the way. Here are some direct quotations from an essay by her:

At Putney, Charles' talent for art found full expression. Those three years were joyous years, the best of his life. His first notable work at

11

Putney was a magic-lantern show called "Anna's Letter." He wrote the story, narrated it on tape with sound by Bartók, and illustrated it by slides with bits of bright paper under glass. . . . It was very effective. . . . Another outstanding effort at Putney was his giant *ABC Book*. A little larger than the *Psalm Book,* it consists of humorous lines and is painted by hand. Charles wanted to print it later, but it never got done. There were so many wonderful plans! At least eight books were lined up. . . .

Charles learned all he knew about printing from his experience as a printer's devil in the office of the *Register-Call* in Central City, Colorado, the summer of 1955 and 1956. The feeling for printer's ink really got in his blood, and he wanted to spend his life printing. To my knowledge, Charles never cut a woodblock in his life until he did the Psalm Book.

This book was his "Senior" project at Putney. He printed it by hand on an old Washington press in Brattleboro, Vermont. It required endless taxi trips into town, and . . . his life's blood went into it. Meals missed, sleep lost trying to keep up a high standard in all subjects, sapped the strength of a boy who was now in the last stages of his illness. The doctors had told me the year before that it was now just a matter of time until he would go. In spite of it all, however, Charles passed his college-board exams in fine style and was given a scholarship at Brown University. He had hoped for Harvard, but that didn't work out.

The last summer was a happy one. Charles worked as an usher in the Central City Opera House, and had a small part in *The Gypsy Baron*. At the same time he was feverishly working to finish a new book of woodblocks about Central City, but unfortunately he was unable to locate the right kind of press for this work, and the book was never finished. As soon as the opera season was over, we moved East. I wanted to be close to Charles, and I had family in Norfolk, Virginia. So we said good-by to the West we loved.

Charles wrote a few enthusiastic gay letters from Brown, but after only six weeks he was taken ill (influenza) and was forced to return to Norfolk after a month in the hospital. He never recovered sufficiently to go on with a work he [had] started in Norfolk. He had discovered, to his delight, an old Washington handpress just like the one he had used in

12

Brattleboro, which he agreed to buy for fifty dollars. The art department of the College of William and Mary in Norfolk agreed to let him set it up there and do his printing. The day before the press was to have been delivered, Charles was taken to the hospital for the last time. . . . [He died on March 7, 1958.]

What a joyous, bubbly person he was—so full of life and enthusiasm. . . .

Charles Knowles' mother, one sees, traveled the whole road with her only son. And her courage was matched only by his.

A sample of his humor and high spirits shows another side of this extraordinary boy:

Putney, February 3, 1956, Dear Mamje, Papji, the Basswelljis and so forth,

When I came back to Putney after vacation, the place was as dry as a piece of Rainbow bread that has been left out for a week. Vermont was the only state in the Union that did not have precipitation during the week before our return.

Here we were, with skis, snowshoes, parkas, boots—and nothing to ski on. Practically everyone in the School was miserable–my roommates were a notable exception. . . . The whole school was praying to St. Peter for snow . . . with no avail till last Monday, when, lo, there came forth a vast abundance of snow from heaven (five inches). And as if that wasn't enough, St. Peter shed his grace again on Thursday with another ten inches . . . [so] since Thursday we have had wonderful skiing. . . . Skiink is here at last!! Zunächst *in defense of books!*

In my opinion (now I *may* be wrong!) . . . books are simply wonderful. They are:

     educational,
     entertaining,
     artistic,
     informative,
     enjoyable,
     etc., etc., etc.

Plizz don't make an inflexible rule about buying books! (i.e., don't).

13

I think that books are too [important] to [be omitted] when economizing.

Although I love books, I don't buy them for the simple enjoyment of buying (even though buying books *is* fun!). I have tried to keep myself to a standing rule that forces me *to read* every book that I buy (exc. Dictionaries and thick ref. bks.). I never buy a book that I only want to read once. . . . Sometimes I may find a book in the library that is so good I *must* have a copy of it. An example of this is the book *The 26 Letters* that I bought while I was still in the sixth grade, and that I still use. . . . [Editor's note: This must have been the source of his manuscript *ABC,* which never was printed.]

Mammy dear, I know your opinions on consistency which are wonderful and should be carried out—except when you have made a judgment that is too quick. . . . This doesn't mean, of course, that if you change your mind I'll go hog wild and buy a lot of books. This simply means that I would like the freedom to buy books if I need them.

I've gotta go, I'se got work. . . .

The letter concludes with an affectionate message, signature, and postscript in mixed German and Russian!

A thirty-five-page essay that Charles Knowles wrote at Putney School in the spring of 1957, at the very time that he was printing his *Psalm Book,* is exceedingly significant. Its title is "As the Hand Turneth: a Study in Creativity."

Creation is a subject very important to me. To make a valuable contribution with my life is the only way that I can assure myself that I have value.

Creation takes inspiration. A creative person must, more than anything else, be a person sensitive enough to receive inspiration and to evaluate it.

Inspiration is an elusive vision. It has to strike the right type of person, at the right time to do its work.

When inspiration strikes a sensitive person at the right time, it is like a drug. It maddens a creative person into activity that cannot stop until the vision that has been seen becomes a reality.

A great artist must have absolutely sure taste, or he will not know how to combine the materials before him into a beautiful whole. . . . [One must] visualize something beautiful clearly enough to be able to select the right materials to carry out [one's] vision.

Death is an overseer. It holds the whip hand that drives men to creation. Few men can honestly reconcile themselves to the fact that they will someday die.

Some people who are skeptical about the after-life because they want to know the truth, still want the reassurance that their lives will have value beyond the present. These are the people who believe that their biographies can assure them of the value of their lives. If they do enough in the time given them, and are lucky enough, they can satisfy themselves that their lives have made a valuable contribution to man.

Whatsoever thy hand findeth to do, do it with all thy might; for there is no work, nor device, nor knowledge, nor wisdom, in the grave, whither thou goest. [Ecclesiastes 9:10]. . . .

In these quotations lies Charles Knowles' epitaph, but his *Psalm Book* of 1957 is his monument. For this single book proves that with the qualities Charles Knowles calls for in his essay on creativity, a great work of art can be achieved by even a seventeen-year-old boy, on his *first* attempt. There are just five essentials: inspiration, integrity, talent, dedication, and—above all—urgency. It is evident from the artist-printer's own words, and from his mother's brief account of his life, that he had each one of these qualities to an astonishing degree.

Some men must spend many years to fulfill a major purpose. A very few who know they live on borrowed time will miraculously achieve as much in a few months. A masterpiece may be a long labor, as in the case of Michelangelo's Sistine Chapel ceiling; or it may be a divine flash, like a short poem by John Keats, who died at twenty-six. Given genius—and that driving sense of urgency—has not Charles Knowles suddenly created a masterpiece on these large sheets of heavy paper, not quite like any other book of our time? How else can one describe the first and last publication of this gallant American youth?

—PHILIP HOFER
Curator of Printing and Graphic Arts,
Harvard College Library

16

the

psalm

book

Blessed is the man that walketh not in the counsel of the ungodly, nor standeth in the way of sinners, nor sitteth in the seat of the scornful.

But his delight is in the law of the Lord; and in his law doth he meditate day and night.

And he shall be like a tree planted by the rivers of water, that bringeth forth his fruit in his season; his leaf also shall not wither; and whatsoever he doeth shall prosper.

The ungodly are not so: but are like the chaff which the wind driveth away.

Therefore the ungodly shall not stand in the judgment, nor sinners in the congregation of the righteous.

For the Lord knoweth the way of the righteous: but the way of the ungodly shall perish.

O Lord our Lord, how excellent is thy name in all the earth! who hast set thy glory above the heavens.

Out of the mouth of babes and sucklings hast thou ordained strength because of thine enemies, thou mightest still the enemy and the avenger.

When I consider thy heavens, the work of thy fingers, the moon and the stars, which thou hast ordained;

What is man, that thou art mindful of him? and the son of man, that thou visitest him?

For thou hast made him a little lower than the angels, and hast crowned him with glory and honour.

Thou madest him to have dominion over the works of thy hands; thou hast put all things under his feet:

All sheep and oxen, yea, and the beasts of the field;

The fowl of the air, and the fish of the sea, and whatsoever passeth through the paths of the seas. O Lord our Lord, how excellent is thy name in all the earth!

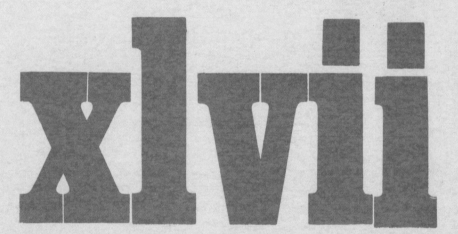

O clap your hands, all ye people; shout unto God with the voice of triumph.

For the Lord most high is terrible; he is a great King over all the earth.

He shall subdue the people under us, and the nations under our feet.

He shall choose our inheritance for us, the excellency of Jacob whom he loved. Selah.

God is gone up with a shout, the Lord with the sound of a trumpet.

Sing praises to God, sing praises: sing praises unto our King, sing praises.

For God is the King of all the earth: sing ye praises with understanding.

God reigneth over the heathen: God sitteth upon the throne of his holiness.

The princes of the people are gathered together, even the people of the God of Abraham: for the shields of the earth belong unto God: he is greatly exalted.

CX

A Psalm of David.

The Lord said unto my lord, Sit thou at my right hand, until I make thine enemies thy footstool.

The Lord shall send the rod of thy strength out of Zion: rule thou in the midst of thine enemies.

Thy people shall be willing in the day of thy power, in the beauties of holiness from the womb of the morning: thou hast the dew of thy youth.

The Lord hath sworn, and will not repent, Thou art a priest for ever after the order of Melchizedek.

The lord at thy right hand shall strike through kings in the day of his wrath.

He shall judge among the heathen, he shall fill the places with the dead bodies; he shall wound the heads over many countries.

He shall drink of the brook in the way: therefore shall he lift up the head.

I will lift up mine eyes unto the hills, from whence cometh my help.

My help cometh from the Lord, which made heaven and earth.

He will not suffer thy foot to be moved: he that keepeth thee will not slumber.

Behold, he that keepeth Israel shall neither slumber nor sleep.

The Lord is thy keeper: the Lord is thy shade upon thy right hand.

The sun shall not smite thee by day, nor the moon by night.

The Lord shall preserve thee from all evil: he shall preserve thy soul.

The Lord shall preserve thy going out and thy coming in from this time forth, and even for evermore.

CXXXVII

A lament in exile.

By the rivers of Babylon, there we sat down, yea, we wept, when we remembered Zion.

We hanged our harps upon the willows in the midst thereof.

For there they that carried us away captive required of us a song; and they that wasted us required of us mirth, saying, Sing us one of the songs of Zion.

How shall we sing the Lord's song in a strange land?

If I forget thee, O Jerusalem, let my right hand forget her cunning.

If I do not remember thee, let my tongue cleave to the roof of my mouth; if I prefer not Jerusalem above my chief joy.

Remember, O Lord, the children of Edom in the day of Jerusalem; who said, Rase it, rase it, even to the foundation thereof.

O daughter of Babylon, who art to be destroyed; happy shall he be, that rewardeth thee as thou hast served us.

Happy shall he be, that taketh and dasheth thy little ones against the stones.

I cried unto the Lord with my voice; with my voice unto the Lord did I make my supplication.

I poured out my complaint before him; I shewed before him my trouble.

When my spirit was overwhelmed within me, then thou knewest my path. In the way wherein I walked have they privily laid a snare for me.

I looked on my right hand, and beheld, but there was no man that would know me: refuge failed me; no man cared for my soul.

I cried unto thee, O Lord: I said, Thou art my refuge and my portion in the land of the living.

Attend unto my cry; for I am brought very low: deliver me from my persecutors; for they are stronger than I.

Bring my soul out of prison, that I may praise thy name: the righteous shall compass me about; for thou shalt deal bountifully with me.

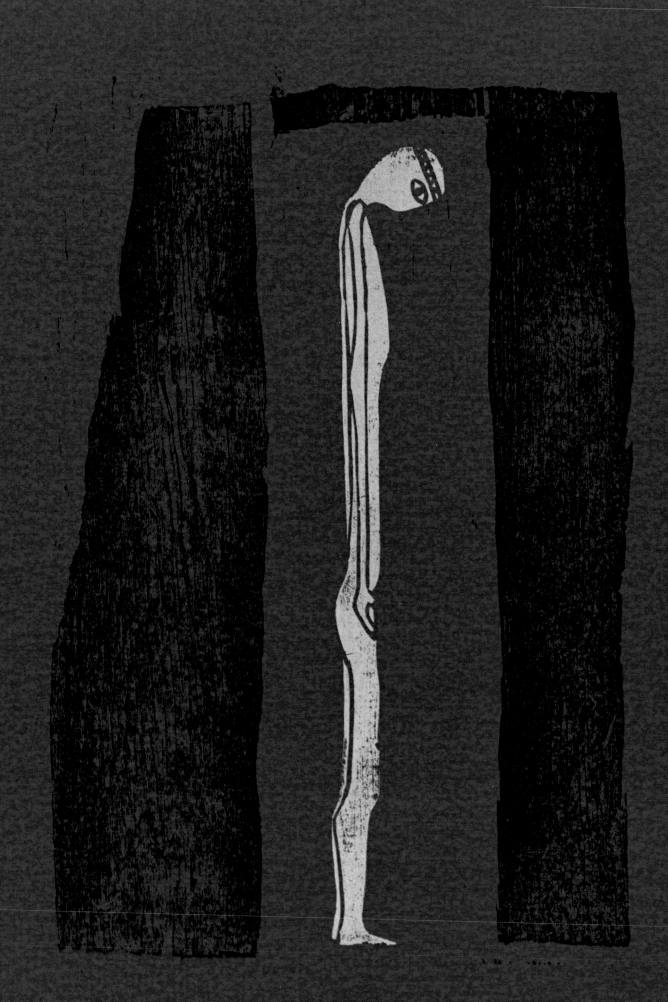

Praise ye the Lord. Praise God in his sanctuary: praise him in the firmament of his power.

Praise him for his mighty acts: praise him according to his excellent greatness.

Praise him with the sound of the trumpet: praise him with the psaltery and harp.

Praise him with the timbrel and dance: praise him with stringed instruments and organs.

Praise him upon the loud cymbals: praise him upon the high sounding cymbals.

Let everything that hath breath praise the Lord.

PRAISE YE the LORD.

ENGRAVED, PRINTED,
& SOLD by
CHARLES KNOWLES,
   printer at the
PUTNEY SCHOOL;
& signed by him:

the psalm book of charles knowles

A Critical Appraisal

In the long history of printing and book illustration in the Western world, summits of achievement stand out, sometimes isolated, sometimes in clearly marked groups, like great rocks and ledges off the New England shore at high tide. Geologically speaking, the northeast coast of America is particularly rich, but in the realm of fine book production neither its short history nor its environment has been very favorable to an art which flourishes best where there has been a long tradition. So it is not surprising that, up till now, American books regarded as works of art have been few, and have almost invariably reflected period styles derived from Europe.

This fact gives peculiar significance to a highly original work by an American artist and printer—the more so since both artist and printer are the same boy. *The Psalm Book* of Charles Knowles appeared very unobtrusively indeed in 1957, since it was "published" in the small community of Putney, Vermont, where the quiet and

37

frugal virtues of our forefathers are still held in high regard. Yet this book is anything but "frugal," and it is more than simply illustrated and printed, as can be seen from its unusual make-up, its varicolored paper, its range of subject and tone—its imagination and force, and the technical accomplishment of its pictures as well as typography.

The first impression is of the original volume's size: 26 by 19⅝ inches—a giant folio for any library shelf! Next, one wonders if it is a book at all; for there is no binding, and the eighteen printed leaves are on heavy paper of varying muted colors. But it *is* a book, having both text and illustration, printed very clearly with good type and huge display letters. These letters are of a heavy "fat-face" variety that were very popular in Europe and America for poster work in the half-century from 1840 to 1890. Yet as they are used here, with few if any capitals, they have a "modern" look. Occasional letters are in color—not black—which illuminates a text page as a splash of brightness lights up a dark painting. Quite certainly, Charles Knowles regarded his text leaves as pictures with organized compositions, considered in close relation to the illustration which occupied the full page opposite. The sheets of paper are printed on one side only, the colors carefully selected to harmonize or contrast with the one which lies next, depending on the over-all effect desired when each pair of sheets, text and illustration, is viewed together. Opening these pairs of sheets, which are blank on the verso, is always a delight; for one never knows what to anticipate in the next double spread.

The title page is extremely simple. There are only the words "The Psalm Book" in large black lower-case display letters, on a soft ruddy ground. This is a serious book, the artist-printer's favorite Psalms from the Bible. Therefore the opening and closing leaves (the latter simply contains the colophon and his signature) are held on a quiet note. But otherwise much of the printing is in color,

38

reflecting the mood of the Psalms, whether joyous, triumphant, devout, sad, or anguished. Eight psalms of striking quality are printed together to match the eight pictures.

How often, in recent times, has an artist been able to represent God in a manner conveying the overwhelming majesty of the Lord, or even an image of Him which carries conviction? William Blake succeeded a number of times, Georges Rouault occasionally, as did one or two others. But, in general, one must go back to a more "believing" era for this—before the tremendous growth of eighteenth-century skepticism. Charles Knowles deliberately depicts God in his illustration for the hundred-and-tenth Psalm: "The Lord said unto my Lord, Sit thou at my right hand. . . . The Lord at thy right hand shall strike through kings in the day of his wrath. . . ." (verses 1 and 5). And his God has the stature, the "gold" majesty, that one would expect beside the much smaller "scarlet" figure of a king. Neither figure is derived from historic European prototypes, though the gestures of both God and king show a knowledge of the Christian symbols. The only noticeable influence is that of primitive art, but so variously and widely drawn that it reveals the original uninhibited vision of Charles Knowles himself.

The eight full-page illustrations are printed from relief blocks designed and cut by the artist, as he states in his colophon. No doubt he mixed the inks himself as well. They are of the most varying shades and colors, covering nearly the whole range of the spectrum. Combined as they are on paper which is also generally tinted, they present striking harmonies or contrasts: dark green, light blue, gray, violet, and yellow; scarlet next to sky blue; light gray and black on deep gray-blue; and many other very interesting color combinations. One can assume that the artist was very experienced with colors indeed, since he is able to be stark, subtle, or sophisticated—sometimes all on the same page.

The illustration to Psalm one (verse 3), with which the volume opens, is perhaps the least technically accomplished of the eight, although the colors of the tree and its fruit are delightfully fresh and well placed. "And he shall be like a tree planted by the rivers of water, that bringeth forth his fruit in his season. . . .") It would seem that the artist was developing his talent to draw and cut his blocks as he progressed with the book! For the illustration to Psalm eight, although better, is also rather naïvely composed: man and his animals placed a bit haphazardly, but with startling clarity, each figure sharply contrasting with the next, and all well drawn. "Thou madest him to have dominion over the works of thy hands. . . . All sheep and oxen, yea, and the beasts of the field. . . ." (verses 6, 7, and 8).

But when one turns the pages to Psalm forty-seven (verse 5) and its illustration opposite, a most sophisticated color scheme and a disarmingly simple representation of the verse are disclosed: "God is gone up with a shout, the Lord with the sound of the trumpet." It is actually the last phrase which is represented on a series of orange and red cloud effects printed over a red paper. Our Lord as "the sound of the trumpet" is a curious, slightly abstract black-hooded figure with a symbolic hunting horn. There is nothing quite like this representation in historic iconography; it must be an invention of Charles Knowles' own.

The illustration of Psalm one hundred and ten (verses 1 and 5) has already been roughly described and commented upon. The figures of God and the king are still more accomplished than those which go before, although one cannot be certain whether the artist designed or cut the various illustrations in their order of sequence as given here, which is the same as that in the Bible.

With the hundred-and-twenty-first Psalm's illustration, the artist's mood changes again, and he renders his first landscape. Also he displays the first influence of his environment: the Vermont hills, in which he then lived, rising in bold tiers of purple above a line of dark trees, and a huge conventionalized red star above it all. "I will lift

40

up mine eyes unto the hills, from whence cometh my help." (verse 1).
It is a wonderfully peaceful American scene, without strong contrasts, and with no figures. But it is entirely convincing despite its
having few lines or contours. Dominating even the hills is the star
of hope called for by the single word "help." Except for the star,
the colors are subdued.

One of the most original color schemes of all is found in the two
facing pages of Psalm one hundred and thirty-seven and its relief-cut
counterpart. The second X of CXXXVII is in yellow, on a gray
page with otherwise very large black letters, which makes a strong
point to hold one's eyes, and to balance the large pictorial composi-
tion that lies on the leaf opposite. Three bright yellow willows, on
which hang violet harps, and a light green river make two horizontal
bands of landscape above the moving group of three dark green bent
human figures roped together under the lash of a slave-driver. "By
the rivers of Babylon . . . they that carried us away captive required
of us a song. . . ." (verses 1 and 3).

Then, like the darkness before dawn—and the Crucifixion before
the Resurrection of Easter Sunday—we have the most powerful
illustration of all. An almost white emaciated naked human figure
stands, head bent, within heavy black walls. "Bring my soul out of
prison, that I may praise thy name. . . ." (Psalm one hundred and
forty-two, verse 7). The paper of the text leaf is gray, the pictorial
leaf a deep gray-blue—like night, and far more beautiful than the
gloom in any prison on earth. Of course, it is the anguish of death
that is thus symbolized immediately before the miracle of the life
hereafter.

The Psalm Book of Charles Knowles ends, as does that of King
David in the Bible, on a note of triumph (Psalm one hundred and
fifty, parts of verses 1, 3, 4, and 6): "Praise ye the Lord—Praise God
in his sanctuary. . . . Praise him with the psaltery and harp . . .
praise him with stringed instruments and organs. . . . Let everything

41

that hath breath praise the Lord. . . ." For opposite this text there are human figures, beautifully draped, in bright and muted colors, each playing an instrument, praising the Lord in his own way. It is not a scene that one will quickly forget, although, like nearly all scenes of rejoicing, it is less immediately dramatic, and far less moving, than the scenes of triumph or of anguish.

The colophon has no illustration and consists of only the lines: "ENGRAVED, PRINTED,/ & SOLD by/ CHARLES KNOWLES,/ printer at the/ PUTNEY SCHOOL;/ & signed by him:/ Charles Knowles./ This is copy number __ of/ ten numbered copies./"

Why were only ten copies printed? The answer is, of course, that these were all the artist-printer had subscriptions or time for, considering the other obligations of his school life and college-board examinations that had to be passed. As it was, it is hard to imagine another school that would have permitted him so much latitude, since he worked virtually alone, with only a little manual-labor help from the art master Jerry Pfohl, and from one classmate-friend, Jon Hendricks, who is now an artist.

Altogether, Charles Knowles' accomplishment is deeply impressive.

—PHILIP HOFER
Curator of Printing and Graphic Arts,
Harvard College Library

Charles Knowles